Your First Book:

The Keys to Successfully Organizing, Writing, and Finishing Your First Book

By Mike D. McLeod

To my wife:

My dreams were kept alive because of your faith and belief in me. Thank you for always speaking life over every situation. Because of you, I have been able to step into the man of God I was always meant to be.

I love you!

Table of Contents

Chapter 1:
Will You Write Your First Book

"The question is: are you willing to take the steps needed to write a book?"

"Man, I want to, but..." There was a long pause. I've had this conversation so many times. I almost knew what was coming. "I just don't know how. I've written so many things in my life, but this seems impossible. As soon as I sit down, it's like my brain goes on strike."

I completely understand why he feels that way. It's challenging to sit down and commit to such a massive undertaking. We have a life outside of writing. Just like I do, this guy has a family. He has a job that he spends 40 hours or more at each week. His children are actively engaged in different activities that keep them running the roads all week long. Proudly chauffeuring his children to these activities takes away some of his time on weekends. He loves it and doesn't want anything to interfere with him being a dad. Eventually, he said the word that every person uses.

"Someday."

When it comes to chasing our dreams, nothing should stand in our way. If that's the case, then why do we use that word "someday" when we are talking about our dreams? It makes me cringe. How many of us could raise our hands and admit to using that word? Here's what it looks like:

"Someday, I will sit down and write my book. So many people will..."

"Someday, I will start that nonprofit because I want to help..."

"Someday, I will start that diet and get in shape."

Our "someday" excuses are holding us back. When it came to *someday* excuses, I was the king of them. I had a legitimate fear of getting out of my comfort zone. There are a lot of things I still struggle with when it comes to seeking out success in different areas of my life. There is an excellent reason why we use these excuses.

It's easy!

I've heard a lot of excuses from people from all walks of life. Of course, I want to be encouraging, but it was reasonably recent when I started hearing excuses everywhere I went. It's not because there's a rise in them. It's because I've become more aware of mine, so it's easier for me to identify that in others.

When it comes to writing, why are so many people so afraid to get started? I mean, people seem to have unbelievable stories to tell that would help the masses. These are stories that are needed; they're stories I would or even need to read. What I've discovered is that most people don't know how to prepare. The writing part isn't that difficult. It's sitting down to write a book that isn't an easy undertaking. If you're not good with computers, then sitting down to create a new software would be near impossible. That's what people are doing when they decide to write a book. They are sitting down in hopes it will just come out without effort. Unfortunately, that's not how it works. I glad it doesn't work that way. It's so much more rewarding to put in the hard work.

When I played basketball, I didn't just run onto the court without preparing. Granted, I was an outstanding player, but to play at my best, I still had to prepare. Although I wasn't a fan of it, I had to stretch. I've always had tight hamstrings, which caused a problem with pain, and to play at my best, I had to stretch more than most people. I had played a lot in my life, so muscle memory had become a thing, too. In other words, there are a lot of parts of basketball that came naturally to me; I kind of did it without thinking. To help combat this, I had to practice during the offseason and mix things up so that my mind, not just my muscles, stayed active. When facing an opponent, I would take time to study that team. I wanted to find every advantage I could to succeed. During those years of playing basketball, I achieved a lot. I have always attributed my success in basketball to my willingness to prepare and put in the work.

I am using my days of playing basketball because I don't see writing, or any other dream your chasing, to be any different. There are a lot of things you need to do to be a success. Being a successful writer, even if you're just writing one book, doesn't happen naturally. You have to put in the proper preparation and work so Your First Book to be the best it can be.

The Never-Ending Rabbit Hole

I tend to become obsessed with things. If I'm into a subject, let's use the brain as an example, then I dive all in. Nothing else outside of that topic exists at the moment. Because of this, I've gained a lot of knowledge. How can that be a bad thing? Well, knowledge isn't a bad thing, but failing to apply that knowledge is devastating. That has always been one of my flaws. I know a lot about a lot, but I use to have a problem applying what I knew.

I mention this because you might have done what I did. We open up the search engine and type something like "how do I write a nonfiction book." An endless list of websites fights for dominance to gain our attention so they can show us how to write our book in 5 easy steps. AND now you can buy this book that goes into further detail to help you find success. Due to my hunger for knowledge, I tend to purchase these books out of curiosity.

The problem today is that we have what's called information overload. I do think there's too much. As I sat down to write a few things, I realized that there were some essential things that people weren't including. I've sought out for a while to figure out why these books or websites on writing were falling short. Don't get me wrong. There is a lot of great information out there. What I am here to do is help you stretch so you can be ready for the game.

I was talking to a friend of mine about the process of writing a legitimate nonfiction book and how intimidating it is. They, just as I have, are used to writing fiction. Stepping into the arena of putting our lives on paper seemed scary. We talked for a while about our little tricks. I say "we," but it was more me talking and her listening intently.

"I feel like you're giving me the cheaters guide to writing," she said with a slight chuckle. "No. I'm serious. Nobody is teaching this. And even if they are, I haven't read it, watched a video about it, or listened to a podcast about it. You've got to put it down."

There you have it. That's how this whole idea came about. Before we fully dive in, I want to be transparent about something. As you read through this little cheaters guide, you'll have moments of thinking, "This sure does seem simple." You know what? It is! That's why I'm baffled that it works so well. I've told several people about these steps, and it's helped them. It would be a shame for me not to share this with everyone because I'm afraid.

I've been afraid to write this for one main reason. I can't believe I'm admitting this, but I've been fearful of the negative reviewers. I know! It seems like a pretty stupid reason not to do something, doesn't it? The steps in this book are going to look so simple that the negative mindset people are going to discredit it. I know this because I've already had people do it that I was trying to help. What I've learned is I can't continue to hold back something that could help 1000's of people just because I'm afraid of a few negative comments.

As you begin this journey, I would encourage you to keep an open mind. I would also ask that you trust me. That might be asking a lot, considering you don't know me. I want you to trust that everything I've included in this book is to help set you up to write the best book possible. Also, be aware that very little of this book will be addressing the writing part. I've learned that proper preparation will allow you to have the performance you're looking for; you're setting yourself up to write a book that will help so many people.

Okay, let's get started. We are first going to dive into the biggest reason why most people fail. It's vital that you have the right mindset when it comes to writing your book.

Chapter 2:
Get Out of Your Head

As I stated at the end of the first chapter, we are going to first delve into what I believe to be the most crucial part of writing a book, your mindset. I'll admit that I will usually find any reason to talk about this subject, but in this case, I have an excellent reason why. My observation has been that people are so in their heads that they'll never be able to accomplish any of their big goals. This tendency to get in their head isn't to discredit their purpose or even their work ethic. Instead, it's to point out that we have a significant problem on our hands when it comes to chasing down and accomplishing our big life goals, especially when it comes to writing a book.

I have one request as we talk about this: please don't just skip this. I know it might not seem like this is that important, but I assure you it is. In the people I've talked to, the number one reason they aren't finishing their writing is because of their mindset towards writing. Some of these people are influential people, too. They've accomplished a lot in their life. However, writing a book requires a whole new level of strength. Usually, they quit long before they're finished. I've done it on a lot of occasions. Then when I attempt to pick it back up at a later time, I find that it's ten times as difficult to write.

I'm a big statistics guy. One has to be careful what they're reading when it comes to statistics, but they do serve a purpose. In this case, I want it to be an eye-opener. Not too long ago, I read an article that claimed 97% of people who start to write a book never finish it. My first response to this was to say it's a bunch of bull. There's no way that can be accurate. Then I remembered the unfinished projects that I have saved. On my external hard drive, I have several books that I started on, but I never even got 10% of the way done.

I've talked to plenty of people who've said they also started on a book. The keyword there is "started." The problem is that they've never even come close to finishing it. The tone in their voice is never one of being proud because they never finished. They're always somewhat ashamed.

(Important reminder: You are NOT a statistic. You have the power to defy the odds! You WILL defy the odds and be proud of what you've accomplished once you've successfully written Your First Book.)

I was talking to a friend of mine at church one day about writing. He began to go through the storyline of what he was writing. As I sat there, I was amazed at all the details he was putting into his character development. Admittedly I started to feel inferior because I tend to write my short stories by the seat of my pants. (Side note: that's a HORRIBLE way of writing.) Then he began to tell me about each book that would come after that. Once again, I was awestruck by the detail that he had put into everything.

"I just like to sit in my chair in my living room and write," he said as he was telling about the series he's writing. "I'm about 75% done with the first book."

"Dude, that's a big deal. Most people never even write that much." Being that I was so excited about what he was describing, the next question seemed natural. "Do you think I could read a couple of chapters? I would love to be one of your proofreaders."

He looked nervous, which I completely understood. It's a scary thing to putting our work into the hands of someone. For me, the feeling of not knowing if they'll like it is incredibly frightening. I reassured him that I was only looking to learn from his writing style.

"Well, I—I haven't materially written anything." He pointed to his temple and said, "It's all up here."

I didn't say anything negative, but I did think not writing anything down was a strange way of being creative. I've wondered a lot since then why he would choose not to. Instead of asking any questions, I would always encourage him as I would pass him at church. That conversation happened ten years ago. A couple of weeks ago, he asked how I was doing. I told him about the books, business, ministry, and everything else going on in my life. I asked him how everything was going with his writing.

"I still haven't gotten around to it." He looked ashamed as he broke eye contact. "It's just that I…"

The rest of what he said isn't as important. Talking to him about his books reminded me of that statistic. So many people never even see their book to completion. That, in my opinion, is heartbreaking. How many people would love to read his series? From what I remember, it's something that he would be proud of publishing. Not everyone can write a fiction novel which such a compelling storyline. I could see someone adapting it into a screenplay that becomes a popular show that is talked about by the masses. In my opinion, he could make a killing by writing that series. While that's not the primary goal of writing (I feel it should be for the love of writing), making a little extra cash from it doesn't hurt either.

Seeing the look on his face made me think about all the unfinished writing goals that people have. I couldn't help but ask a few questions. Why aren't they writing? Why aren't they finishing what they write? What is causing them to accept defeat so willingly?

When I began plotting out this book, I tried looking up the source of the 97% statistic. I couldn't find it, which is disappointing, but what was more alarming is the claim that only 20% of the people who do write a book publish it. Wait! Like what?!?! How is that even possible?

While I'm sure there are a lot of other things that come into play, I have a few reasons why someone might not finish their book. Although I'm not proud of this, I feel like I was the master with some of the things that hold people back. You see, I have firsthand experience in not getting things done. I was one of the worst at one time. The reasons why I feel some people won't finish what they started are procrastination, feeling like it needs to be perfect, waiting for the proper time/market, and suffering from writer's block. Each one of these has affected me personally and know how crippling it can be. Let's first address what's been my biggest hurdle to get over, procrastination.

Procrastination

More times than I can count, I've heard people say, "I'm a procrastinator by nature." That's something I've said before. I adopted the fact that it was a part of who I was. There are a lot of reasons why it's dangerous to choose this as being a part of us. Before we get into the specifics, let me clear up one major misconception about procrastination. Procrastination is not an innate characteristic; it's a learned behavior.

Imagine taking your newborn baby into the doctor for its first visit. The baby has done well since being out of the hospital. They're regularly feeding, gaining weight appropriately, and their color is looking fantastic. Everything, from your perspective, seems to be perfect. The doctor puts your baby on the scale, and everything looks good. Next, they check all the vitals and everything else required to ensure your baby is healthy. The doctor runs through everything, and you, as new parents, are beaming with joy.

"The only problem that I see is," the doctor pauses and has a worried look on his face. "It seems as if your baby struggles with procrastination. I'm going to have to refer you to a specialist."

The parents look at each other with tear-filled eyes as the mother says, "How can this be? Not our baby! Why?"

This scenario seems ridiculous because it is. We would never accept a doctor, or anyone else, claiming our beautiful baby is a procrastinator. Yet, we willingly accept this as being a part of who we are. There are plenty of people who've studied procrastination over the years. Research has shown that it can cause health problems. Those health problems include anxiety, severe clinical depression, obsessive-compulsive disorder (OCD), and attention deficit disorder, just to name a few. Because I struggled with procrastination, I have personally experienced some of these things at one point.

Why? That's the question I've had a lot as I thought about writing this book.

Why are people so willing to adopt it if it's such an issue? Why would someone be willing to spiral down a path of destruction for the sake of being a procrastinator? Allow me to use my life as a way to shine a light on one of my reasons why.

When I was growing up, I discovered real quick that I was the smart kid. I didn't have to study. Because of this, I developed some bad habits. Two of the worst habits I developed is I barely did enough to get by, and I waited until the last minute to do my homework or project. These two things didn't seem like a big deal at the time. Why would it? It's only high school. Let's fast forward a little bit.

I became an adult and chose not to go to college. You know...because, why would I do that. Deep down, I knew that I was smart enough to figure things out on my own. Boy, was I wrong! I had plenty of chances to be successful. The problem is that I had become one of the world's worst procrastinators. Most of the time, I would wait until the last minute to do things, but it was usually too late. I would have underestimated the work that was required, so I made excuses. "Life is just unfair," I would tell people. "Every time I have the chance to get ahead, it's like life rips the carpet from under me. Why do I even try?"

I had created a habit. To one degree or another, we are all a product of our environments. Mine was one of my choosing, even if I didn't know I was doing it. By choosing to be lazy in school, I was creating a habit of not doing the work. My brain was wiring itself to react in a certain way. My procrastination was my own doing, and it almost ruined me. That's why I am talking about it because I've seen it more than anything.

Another reason why people procrastinate is that they have dealt with a few things that weren't their fault. I have talked to a few people who suffered from some severe trauma. It wasn't something they chose. Naturally, this causes fear, which leads to procrastinating. In the end, and I know it sucks to hear this, we are the ones still choosing to accept procrastination as our constant companion.

What I include in the rest of this book are tools to help you fight through this. I know what it feels like to be a victim to it, but I also know what it feels like to kick procrastination in the butt. Trust me when I say it's not as difficult as you think to get up and write your book. You're going to conquer it and change some lives in the process. You can change adopted behaviors. That's excellent news.

Feeling Like it Needs to be Perfect

As stated before, only 30% of people who've completed writing a book publish it. This one baffled me at first. Then I recalled a conversation I had with someone about a month ago. They told me that they had two completed books they wanted to publish. Curiosity kicked in, and I needed to know why they weren't going to publish it.

"I need to go back through it and make sure everything's where it needs to be," they said with hesitance. After a few moments, they concluded by saying, "I think at this point that's become more of an excuse than anything."

I told them the statistic I had just heard, and they said they believe it 100%. I also know this one from personal experience. I think that what you write will never indeed be perfect. The problem with perfect is that you'll never achieve it. All of us have heard the saying that we are our own worst enemy. That is a true statement, especially when it comes to writing your book.

I can't answer for everyone, but for me, there is a legitimate fear that enforces my need for perfection. Most people I know are afraid to put their completed work in the hands of others. It's a little strange because the end goal is to put it in the hands of thousands. The dominating fear for me was that when I put it in the hands of others, they will annihilate what I wrote. They will see my grammar as being too elementary and, for some reason, will find a way to make me the poster child for "adults that aren't allowed to write a book ever again."

Another reason why perfection is such a problem is because of our social standards. We live in a culture that only posts the *perfect* picture. The picture we see will be one of about 30 that the person took. We read stories from our friends on social media about their *near-perfect* families. Even their not-so-good moments or funny moments seem *perfect.*

We also have open access to millions of books through online platforms. We can go to the library (yes, those are still a thing) and check out whatever we want. We read through other people's books and think they're *perfect.* I read about 50 books a year. I can find plenty of errors in every book I read. It's odd that even with those errors, I still have this picture of *perfection* that is crippling me.

Here is what I have learned: you'll never achieve perfection. What you can achieve is good enough.

I know that sounds like an insult, but I assure you it's not. Some of my favorite books of all time have grammatical errors that make me wonder how everyone missed them. At the end of rereading those books, I will smile and be thankful I invested the time to read them. At some point, the authors had to decide that what they had in front of them was good enough. Good enough isn't bad. Some of the greatest classics written were by authors who had to reach a "good enough" moment.

Get perfect out of your mind. It lowers the bar and makes your dreams achievable. Typing that just now made me giggle. Could you imagine seeing that on a motivational poster? Pictured would be a guy jumping hurdles, but the hurdles are only two feet high. In big, bold print below that picture, it says, "Lower your goals, and you'll achieve whatever you want." Lowering your goals is not what I'm asking you to do. Your goal is to write the best book possible. What I'm trying to get you to see is that the "best book possible" isn't going to be perfect. It just won't. By getting perfect out of your mind, you'll find it easier and more enjoyable to write.

Waiting for the right time or market

You know what? I am going to make this one super easy for you. NOW is always the right time to write and publish your book. I am in an author's Facebook group. Most of the people in this group are new authors. While I understand having questions about the process, I feel the timing questions don't make sense. The vast majority of nonfiction authors aren't just writing something relevant right now; they're writing something will continue to be relevant years from now. Waiting on the *perfect* time or market isn't something to consider. NOW! Write and publish your book now!

As I type this, there is a virus that has made headline news all over the world. Most of the world is stuck in homes waiting for just a little good news. If you're looking to write a book on that, then right now is a perfect time. However, most people aren't seeking to write things like that that are time-sensitive. I think the book *How to Win Friends and Influence People* by Dale Carnegie is a perfect example of the point I am trying to make. His book hit the shelves in October of 1936. Yes, there are a few outdated things, but the book still sells about 250,000 books a year. That book is just as relevant today as it was in 1936.

Don't let timing be the reason you're not writing your book. Let's be honest with each other right now. Most likely, if you're using that as an excuse, then you're trying to find any reason not to write your book. Let's call it what it is. You're scared. Well, stop letting fear dictate your future and the influence you could have.

Writer's Block

Writer's block. Look at those intimidating words. Does it make you quake in your boots? The scary monster writer's block is a lot of people's familiar companion. Everyone at one point or another has struggled with writer's block. It's something that will bring up almost 19 million results on a search engine. I've talked about this stupid topic more than any other because it's one of my problems. And yes, I think it's ridiculous.

Let me help you understand what writer's block is. It's an excuse. That's all it is. How do I know this? I allowed it to be a thing that crippled me for a few years. Yes, I wrote a few things here and there. There was nothing significant that came from that season of my life, though.

There are a few things that caused my writer's block:

- Physical fatigue (creates a mental rats nest of chaos)
- Fear of rejection (this was one of my main reasons)
- Laziness (it took me years to admit that I was lazy)
- Lack of structure

Everyone has their reason for struggling with writer's block. Not too long ago, I had someone argue with me saying that they were no longer creative. They believed they had gone through far too many trials in their life and that somehow stripped them of all creativity. I know this is just a poor excuse to make failure easier to swallow. I wait for the perfect moment to "changed the subject," so I can see how they would respond. I've done this several times to multiple people.

"Wow! That's crazy," I will interrupt while looking at my phone. "My sister just texted me and said the lottery is at $352 million. Dang, can you imagine what it would be like to win that much money? What would you do with all that?"

The rest of the conversation is predictable. Whoever I'm with will begin to tell me everything they would do with this imaginary money that they're not going to win. A detailed plan will unfold without much thought. I will ask them open-ended questions to engage them further. What I am doing is getting them to engage their imagination.

"You know what you just did?" A huge smile will come across my face as I continue, "You just used your imagination about something that isn't even going to happen. You don't have that money, yet you know everything you're going to do with it. You know how you will help your church, your family, your community, and so much more. That, my friend, is called using your imagination. Now, let me show you how to write that book."

The point is that writer's block doesn't have to be a thing. Elizabeth Gilbert, the author of *Eat, Pray, Love,* said, "I don't sit around waiting for passion to strike me. I keep working steadily because I believe it is our privilege as humans to keep making things. Most of all, I keep working because I trust that creativity is always trying to find me, even when I have lost sight of it."

Heres a fact: writer's block can be conquered instead of it being a poor excuse, which is all it is at best.

A little later in this book, I will arm you a few things that will help you stay ahead of writer's block.

<u>Mindset is everything!</u>

At one job I worked at, there was a phrase plastered to my supervisor's office wall. It said, "Proper preparation prevents poor performance." It's the 5 P's, and it's perfect for what you're trying to accomplish. When I asked him about it, he made it very clear that he prepared for success long before it physically got to him. Do you know what I learned about that guy? He was incredibly successful in almost everything he did. Even in his "failures," he found success because he allowed those failures to teach him something.

The 5 P's always stuck with me. Proper preparation is key to the success of writing Your First Book. With proper preparation in mind, I need to cover a few final things. Don't worry; it will be quick.

The point of this chapter was to point out that the excuses we make cripple us instead of helping us. I hope that you would read all of it and see that there is another option. You CAN be successful. You WILL be successful. No longer do you have to adopt procrastination, perfection, timing, or writer's block as being a part of who you are. If you chose those learned behaviors over time, then you can unlearn them and replace them with healthier habits. The mindset you adopt before you even put pen to paper is vital to your success. Most of what I learned is that we, the potential authors of the world, have to power to achieve success by properly setting ourselves up.

For years I struggled with crippling depression. I've read the books, talked to the right people, and said all the positive affirmations. Where everything changed was *how* I said and looked at those affirmations. In your mind, you have to get excited and *feel* what you're saying. As you think about writing your book, try to imagine it completed. Close your eyes and use your real emotions to *feel* what it would be like holding it in your hand. Imagine how you would feel handing it to someone in your life that you love. Why does this work? Your brain doesn't know how to interpret that as real or fake. All it knows is that it *feels* like you just did something amazing. Doing this will begin to physically wire your brain for success long before you achieve it.

By changing how you think, you will help you learn to chill out when you hit your first major roadblock. By the way, you 100% will run into a roadblock along the way. By being prepared for it, you won't allow yourself to get down and quit like 97% of the people.

One of the roadblocks I hit was remembering certain things about my past. I would focus on missed opportunities, costly mistakes, and so much more. I allowed my past to beat me up. Now I use it as a lesson to learn from, and it continues to propel me into a brighter future. Not using it as a lesson crippled me, which lead to procrastination, and everything else we've already covered.

Don't allow your past to dictate your present circumstances, which in turn will dictate how your future turns out. I know this might seem like a bunch of nonsense, considering we are only talking about writing a book. I assure you this will change your writing life forever. I guess the biggest lesson in all of this that I can teach you, the one thing that will help you retrain your brain is that you have to be confident. Confidence is critical in anything you do. Confidence will continue to grow stronger if you feed the right thoughts and starve the bad habits.

I once played against another basketball player who statistically was far better than I was. For weeks I dreaded the upcoming game because I liked being one of the best on the floor. I didn't want him to dominate me. About a week before the game, I started thinking about ways I could get in his head. I studied his every move on the tapes we received. (Yes, this was in the days of videotape.) I went to one of their games so I could watch him in person. I made my presence known. When we played, it wasn't easy to dominate, but my new confidence was evident. That ended up being the only game where I scored a triple-double. I got double digits (10+) in blocks, points, and rebounds. That was also the opponent's worst game.

I am not trying to toot my own horn (but dang it feels good to do it). What I want you to see is that mindset is everything. Before that game, that guy appeared to be better than me. On the tape, in person, and on paper, he was better in every way. Due to adequately preparing, physically, and mentally, I was able to show off more than I had ever done before. It felt good.

Writing Your First Book is going to feel good. It's going to be worth working through all the obstacles that present themselves to you.

What I want for you is to adopt a new mindset that you will dominate the process of writing a book. Of course, it won't be easy. I don't think it's easy for the vast majority of authors out there. However, by working on your mental game, you are changing how your brain responds to the process of everything. You will win!

Now that you're getting your mind right, the next chapter will go into detail about what it takes to set yourself up physically to win.

Chapter 3:
Set Yourself Up to Win

In the last chapter, we discussed one of my favorite topics, the power of the mind. Now we are diving into the idea of what it takes to set yourself up to win. Most people, including myself for longer than I'd like to admit, don't grasp the importance of adequately preparing. I believe we can implore a few little things that help us stay on task. As stated before, staying focused and fighting off writer's block is something that affects all of us. I want to share a few things with you that will help you immensely.

As I sat down to write this chapter, I couldn't help but think about Kobe Bryant. At the moment of writing this, his death is still fresh on everyone's memory. It came as a shock to everyone, including me. I remember when he first came into the league. Being such a massive Michael Jordan fan, I hated hearing about this kid who came straight from high school. How could so many people compare him to the greatest player of all time? Since his death, I have watched hours of interviews and heard a lot of stories. There were a lot of things that set him apart from everyone else in the league. He wasn't going to be outworked by anyone.

Most people should have an idea of who Kobe is. We all get to hear these beautiful stories, but what if they were a little different? What if our memory of him was tainted? Hang with me for a second. Imagine your watching Kobe in the biggest game of the year. The Lakers are preparing to play for the championship. As he steps onto the court to warm up, a reporter steps up to do the pregame interview.

"Kobe, what did you do to prepare for the game today? Are you at all nervous?"

With a slight chuckle, Kobe says, "Well, I don't prepare. I make sure the rest of the team is working out, but I don't have to. I'm naturally gifted; I don't have to work out."

The reporter, along with everyone watching, would lose interest in his game. Yes, we would have still loved the skill at which he played, but something would be lost. Why didn't we ever hear stories like that about Kobe? The reason is that he worked out longer and harder than anyone else on the team. He didn't just play with a rare intensity; he also practiced with that same intensity. Kobe did whatever it took to set himself up to win at anything he did at life.

People who are the most successful in life are usually the people who worked harder and smarter than everyone else. They set themselves up to win. Setting ourselves up to win is something that we, as writers, should do. There are a few things I've done and taught others to do that have proven to help. We are going to go over the biggest ones.

Location, location, location

There is a battle that rages on when it comes to choosing the perfect location to write. Ultimately it boils down to deciding whether to write in public or in private. As I was researching for this, the search engine showed thousands upon thousands of articles from people claiming that writing in public is a healthy option. When I looked this up, I was expecting to find tons of people agreeing with me. I've always taken a pretty strong stance in that we should always choose a private location to write.

When it comes to writing in public, a lot of people will choose a cute cafe somewhere. They will sip on some coffee and start working. Due to being a professional people watcher, I've noticed something. These people spend the majority of their time looking up. Their attention isn't on what they're working on, their writing. If writing in public is such a good thing, then why are they so distracted. I just can't see how having such a distracted mentality could be conducive to any kind of growth.

Not too long ago, someone told me that they "need those distractions." I stared at them for a moment, and the look on my face must have confirmed what I was thinking. What I wanted to say was, "You're an idiot!" Instead of belittling him, I chose to congratulate him on his writing, but I offered him a challenge. I briefly went over the things I'm covering in this chapter. He said he would give it one week and let me know how it worked out. In the end, he got a lot more work done, further proving my point that writing in public isn't the greatest idea. I do believe we need an occasional break from our usual writing spot. However, I don't think it should come with the ever-mounting distractions that come with writing in a public place. At the very least, don't try to write your rough draft in public. My reasoning for this stance is that we can't afford distractions.

My stance has always been that we need a place of our own, space specifically carved out just for your work. Our area can be a small desk (end table with a chair) that is against a wall of the living room or dining room.

I've noticed in my own life how my brain associates this workspace.
When I have a space that is strictly for work, I don't get as distracted. My brain has locked into place that my desk is a place of work. I've tried to write outside of that, and it doesn't work as much. That desk is my "office" in my home. You will find that you're not as distracted when you've created a space to work. Allow me to give you a glimpse into my life and why this works.

My wife and I have a litter of children and another on the way. The two youngest are extremely loud. I don't currently have the luxury of having an office in the house. We need every room to help house our small army. My desk is now in the dining room. It is off-limits to everyone, and that includes my wife. You might be thinking that sounds harsh. The thing is that everyone is okay with it. In their minds, there was never an option to use my desk for anything else. My office (aka desk) is for me to get my work done.

One day we had a family friend come over. He had a few things in his hand and went to set it on my desk. One of the kids quickly said, "You can't put anything on there. That's his desk." They didn't say this out of fear. It was quite funny. My daughter said it with a tone that kind of questioned why he would do such a thing. Why? Because that's my space. Because of this, I'm able to jump right into work mode whenever I need to.

Another thing to take note of is that everyone respects the fact that I'm working. Most of the time, nobody in the family just walks up to start talking to me. They leave me to my work. Maybe this seems rude to some people, but we see it as my work. I am dedicating time to writing so I can help people and make a living at the same time. One of my jobs is being an author. I write. My desk is where I write. I have a sign that I hang when talking to me isn't allowed. It says, "Do not disturb. Genius at work. Thanks."

I believe setting yourself up with a workspace will allow you to get more work done. If you're in the house with other people, then help them understand that your "desk" is your workspace. Set the precedent that your desk is strictly for you. Using your workspace for other things isn't usually a good idea, either. Your work area is for work-related matters.

By taking such a strong stance on this, you're also setting the standard for you. Mentally you're telling yourself how important your work is. I don't know why this works, but it does. Taking a firm stance with having a dedicated work area has worked for plenty of other people I've helped. Taking this stance can't work if you're going to a public place to work. I've never been successful walking into the cafe and saying, "Excuse me, sir. But this table belongs to me when I'm working." I'm reasonably sure that it would end very badly for me.

Find yourself a place to write. Trust me! You're setting yourself up to win—every little thing matters.

<u>I love rewards!</u>

All of us are creatures of habit. If we aren't used to writing, then it becomes challenging to stay on track. Eventually, we will hit a huge mental roadblock and not know what to do. Now that you've set yourself up with an area to work from, it's time to talk about rewards.

Most writers frequently miss this simple step. I've talked to plenty of writers, musicians, and business owners who have never even considered the concept of rewarding themselves for what they've accomplished. It's my view that rewards can make a massive difference in the way we retrain our daily habits.

Recently a person I talked to honestly believed that rewards are too self-centered. She didn't think the rewards were healthy. When she said this, I didn't respond appropriately. I laughed out loud. Thank God she knew me well enough and wasn't offended in any way. I have a good reason why I laughed. Rewarding ourselves for the work we are doing isn't selfish. It helps motivate us. Allow me to take a page from my life once again.

I was young and working in a call-center. The department I worked in was technical support for cellular service. Maybe you don't know a lot about technical support, but it's not a lot of fun. Usually, it's taxing for every person from management down. The reason is that nobody is ever calling into a call-center to tell the operator how well they're doing. It is almost always a complaint. Although it wasn't a requirement, we were always encouraged to go for the upsell. Few people in technical support ever did that.

As an incentive, the company rolled out a commission plan for those in our department. It didn't seem like a lot of extra money, but the keyword there is "extra." I could do whatever I wanted with the extra. I adopted a mindset that the extra would go towards something I wanted. Seeing this as extra was brilliant because it meant I didn't have to spend my regular check, which I wouldn't have done anyway. I now had a reward in front of me.

A couple of people I worked with got together one day and decided to have a competition. We wanted to see who could sell the most extras. I printed out two pictures, a picture of a freestyle BMX bike, and a surround sound system for my living room. I was known for calming the angriest of customers. I quickly incorporated selling into my way of helping them. It wasn't as difficult as everyone else made it. In the end, I sold ten times more than anyone else. We ended up selling so much that the company had to redesign the commission plan. We made "too much," and they didn't want to keep doing that. Something positive came from this, though.

Someone within corporate flew down to talk to me about what I had done. The corporates were curious as to how I was able to sell so much. I was in the top 10 in sales in the company. Those stats included customer service and stores. Somehow I had sold more than the people who had the job of selling every day. I walked them over to my desk and showed them the pictures. I had added a few other things to my goal.

"It's easy," I said to Mr. Big Wig. "These are all the things I want to buy. I buy those things with the commission. Because it's in my line of sight, I can't forget why I'm selling."

Taking that approach to sales seemed like common sense to me, but apparently, it was groundbreaking to everyone else. They went back to corporate and worked on a new campaign. Instead of money, we would have points. These points could buy things in an online store. While others found a reason to complain, I got excited. I ended up getting so much stuff I was asking other employees what they wanted. I stayed in the top 10, and people throughout the entire company knew my name.

What I am trying to tell you is that having a reward system in place is a good thing. But how, you may be asking, am I supposed to that with writing? I believe there are two types of rewards that will help you through your journey of writing.

Firstly, you need to look at the short term game. What can you do to help you every day you sit down to write? Having a small reward along the way helps keep you motivated. It can be something incredibly simple, but that's okay. But remember, this reward is something you should enjoy while you're working on your book. You can't partake of whatever your reward is any other time. So choose wisely. Maybe you like a specific beverage or candy. Decide that you will only enjoy that while you're writing. Doing this is like saying to your brain, "Good job, brain! We crushed it today! Let's do this again tomorrow."

For my small reward, I choose something that everyone else in the house thinks is disgusting. Guess what? That doesn't matter, and it works to my advantage. My "disgusting" reward is that I have a legitimate love for soft licorice from all over the world. I'm not talking about the cheap American junk that you get in Walmart, either. I've never said this before, but I guess I'm a licorice snob. I've discovered that most people loathe licorice. My great-grandmother, who I also considered a friend, loved licorice. For some reason, I fell in love with it, too. We would sit on the porch swing and eat it while we watched the cars pass. Because it brings me good memories, I've adopted this as being one of my short term rewards. Every day that I sit down to write, I will allow myself to have a few pieces of licorice. There is a brand from Australia that is WONDERFUL! Licorice might not seem like a big deal to you, but it works for me.

The next thing you need to have is the final reward. This reward is a lot bigger than your daily reward. Having a bigger reward helps keep you motivated on the days when the small reward just isn't enough. Some would argue that finishing is rewarding enough. Those people aren't exactly wrong, but why not add a bonus? It's your life. Reward yourself on a job well done! Maybe you and your significant other want to go on a day trip that you usually wouldn't take. Do it! Find something that isn't very common for you to do and choose that as a reward.

For my example, I am going way back. I went to a private school in the '90s. There was a work program at the school that allowed me to work off my tuition. My parents didn't force me to do this. I chose to do this on my own. The work we did during the summer was hard. For me doing it was easy. There was a massive payoff in the end. Once I'd finished my summer, I would have worked off most of my tuition. Also, making my school a better place, as cheesy as that might sound, was my payoff. Even knowing I had helped my parents was a big deal for me, too. I always kept that end goal in front of me. My reward was being able to go to school, knowing I chose to invest in my future.

At first, I thought my school story wasn't the best example. I still remember the feeling of knowing my hard work had paid off. I didn't have a lot of ways to reward myself. So I took whatever I could to put in front of me. Whatever the payoff is should be something that keeps you motivated. The payoff for me was an emotional one. I loved that school more than anything. So working toward that bigger reward felt right to me.

Your payoff, that big reward should motivate you. Put up a picture of whatever it is you want to do. I am a massive advocate of vision boards. While this isn't an actual vision board, it works in the same way. It's best to keep something in your face that will help pep you up when you're feeling defeated and want to quit. Finished your book will be the most excellent feeling, but that's not always enough. For a lot of people, that's not tangible enough. That's why having a big reward will set you up for success.

Get hyped

One of the things I've learned through the years is that every tool helps. I loved to get hyped about sitting down to write. For me, this comes in two parts. I will be the first to tell you that most don't choose to incorporate what I'm sharing with you. My experience has taught me that this works. We've all heard the phrase, "If it's not broke, don't fix it." Well, this works for more than just me. Getting hyped comes in two parts: getting the blood flowing and the right music.

Getting the blood flowing isn't something most people think about when they're going to write a book; it's not on a checklist of things to do. The idea of getting my blood pumping came to me one day unexpectedly. I was reading a book by Dr. Amen, who is an expert in the area of neuroscience. He, as well as plenty of other neuroscientists, stresses that exercise is essential for proper brain health. I think most of us know this, but allow me to give you a little information that will help you. Please don't skip ahead or tune me out. I promise there is a significant reason for including this.

When you exercise, you're allowing the blood to carry more oxygen to your body more rapidly. The human brain uses about 20% of the oxygen that your blood carries. That means your brain can strengthen the things that help it fire more rapidly and effectively. The fact is that exercise allows your brain to accomplish more. Why is this important to writing? That's easy! The better your brain operates, or fires off the signals, the better you'll be able to stay focused. You'll be able to finish your book quicker than most people. In the process, you'll be helping your body, too. Talk about a winning combination.

How do we incorporate this into our writing?

Doing simple exercises for a couple of minutes before writing will get your blood flowing. Sometimes I choose to dance. Granted, I do this when nobody is at home, but it works. I will pull up a dance aerobics video and dance for a few minutes. I don't know if I can call it dancing. My dancing and walking into a spiderweb sure do look a lot alike.

Nonetheless, I will do this and feel great while doing it. I love it. Exercising leaves me feeling gross and sweaty, so I take a quick shower. With my water for hydration in hand, I will sit down and start writing. Getting that little bit of exercise seems to work wonders for my creative brain, and I discovered this by accident.

I've been struggling with some severe health issues. Due to these health problems, I've been down and unable to do the things I used to. Being without a traditional job is when laziness kicked in. To my defense, I didn't mean for it to happen. I didn't even notice it was happening for a long time. I was working on a book but was having trouble getting up and staying focused. I had my goals in place, but I was falling short. Out of frustration one day, I started punching the air. Like out of a boxing movie, there I was giving it all I had. I jumped around and just enjoyed the moment. Maybe it was a moment of insanity? I don't know. All I know is that I wrote more that day than I had written in a long time.

Some kind of daily exercise is vital to your mental health, which in turn affects the way you write. Maybe you can't do a lot physically. I get it. Get up and go for a walk around your yard. Sometimes I get up and pace around the house for about 20 minutes while listening to a podcast. Other times I will walk around my neighborhood. Walking is simple but effective. It's a super healthy way to get your heart rate up. That is my primary source of cardio, and it's helping. You'll feel better overall, but you'll also notice that you're able to be more productive.

Let's talk about the tunes

The next thing that helps with getting hyped is proper music. Before I briefly cover this, I want you to know that my stance on this isn't too popular. When I looked for information on music while working, almost every article I found advised against it. With that in mind, I will say that this might not work for you. However, I believe that people aren't utilizing music properly. I'm hoping you'll be on the same page as me as I further explain.

When it comes to listening to music, I've learned that most people choose a playlist of their favorite music. My issue with this is that most people end up distracted. Once upon a time, I did the same thing. I would turn on a playlist with my favorite groups. Not too long into writing, I would find myself distracted and quitting the project in front of me. I used the excuse that I wasn't feeling creative or blamed it writer's block. The truth is that my music was a distraction. I had to find a way to fight this because I needed my music.

You've set yourself up with a spot to work out of, but maybe you're like me in that almost anything is distracting. How do we drown out the noise and stay focused at the same time? A lot of us need music to help drown out the world around us. I was desperately trying to figure this out a few years ago when I accidentally figured out a solution. Mentioning this might date me a little, but this happened at the height of dubstep. Dubstep is a style of techno music. I love the way it sounds. I usually try to find the ones that have no words. Words are distracting, and I don't like the excessive profanity anyway. While listening to a dubstep playlist, I noticed that I was extremely focused. I also saw that I was writing quickly. That's when I realized that lyrics, or the lack thereof, mattered.

Since then, I've added several playlists as my favorites, depending on the mood of what I'm writing. I write a lot of fictional short stories. Each one has its feel, so I will choose a playlist that reflects what I am writing. It has made a significant difference in my writing.

About a month ago, I needed something that had a warrior sound to it. I wanted to have words, too. Remember that this is distracting. Well, I found a workaround for this. Finding music from other countries works very well. I ended up stumbling upon The HU. They're a Mongolian metal band who has moved up to my top 10 favorite bands. I can't understand a word they're saying, but listening to their music makes me happy and puts me in the proper mood when I need it to write.

A few of the other playlists are dubstep Don, yodeling (one-time use so far), suspenseful instrumental, intense orchestra, and eerie instrumental (I use this one more than all the other combined). I would encourage you to venture out and find a style of music that fits what you're doing. Right now, I'm listening to dubstep to help keep me pumped up as I write. You'll find that music helps you stay focused if appropriately used. As a bonus, you might find a few groups or styles of music you never knew existed. I choose world music more than music in English.

Find your why

We have discussed a few things that will help you get in the groove of writing. You have a space set aside, we know what you're rewards are going to be, are incorporating some physical activity to get the blood pumping, and maybe have a playlist or two that will help you stay hyped. I love these things and believe they'll play a significant role in you finding success in writing. What we will discuss now is what I consider the most important tool to help you be successful. When I say "successful," I am talking about every area of your life.

This might be the first time I've written the next sentence. I've saved the best for last. Like in the infomercials, this is my "but wait...there's more" moment. The "more" I'm referring to is finding our why.

Over the last few years, I've discovered that having a purpose for what we do is one of the most important keys to success. I've spent most of my life coming in the last place in everything. My mentality was mostly negative. Because of this, I never achieved anything significant. I was looking at my goals and feeling like they were always getting farther and farther away. There were plenty of tears that flowed as I looked at those goals. I almost accepted that I would never find success, that somehow I was forever doomed to be this failure. That's when I sat down and started writing in my journal. A couple of questions came out of that moment.

"Why do I have those goals?"
"Why is it important for me to finish what I've started?"
"Why should I keep dreaming big?"

Those questions had a common denominator, and it's one word. "Why" is what I kept asking. It started as a way to feel bad about myself, but it became a healthy set of questions. That's when I realized that the rewards, the setup, everything else was pointless if I didn't know the reason why I was doing what I was doing. I sat down and wrote a mission statement for the first project on my list. There were plenty of down moments. Remember, I was undoing a lifetime of negative programming. It wasn't easy to rid myself of those things that adopt a positive mindset. That's when things began to change.

Having a mission statement is one of the most important things you can do for yourself. I have a personal mission statement for my life, for each time I sit down to write something, and for any other big life-changing moment. Mission statements are something most successful people have. I didn't know this for a long time. It was while talking to a pastor friend of mine that I realized how important they are. He casually threw his family mission statement out as if it were nothing. Their family mission statement was something he knew by heart. It was personal. It had significant meaning. Consequently, he does everything in his life with intentionality. What they do in his family, no matter what it is, seems always to be aligned with that mission statement.

In his book, *The 7 Habits of Highly Effective People,* Stephen Covey said, "The most effective way I know to begin with the end in mind is to develop a personal mission statement or philosophy or creed." This quote is coming from an author who wrote a book that has sold more than 10 million copies. I think this guy knows what he is talking about when it comes to accomplishing goals. A lot of successful people acknowledge that book as one of the must-reads if you're going to find success.

I can't tell you what your mission statement should be. What I know is that it should be personal. There are a few things I want to always focus on in my life. I want Jesus Christ to be at the helm of everything I do. I want to create a family legacy that lasts through generations. I want to help as many people in this world to become better versions of themselves as possible. Those are a few things I include when I am working on a mission statement.

When writing your mission statement, I believe it's essential to include things that make it very personal. The reason why you want to make it personal is that it's easier to attach your emotions to it. When a person connects their emotions to something, it becomes deeply embedded in their mind. The creation of strong neural connections, which is what those positive emotions will do, is what will make the long hours and frustrations worth it.

The beauty of a mission statement is that it will make the obstacles easier to handle. There is a myriad of tremendous obstacles that my family has faced over the last two years. Through most of it, I've remained strong. There were a few moments of weakness, but overall I couldn't forget my mission statement. No matter what the obstacle was, it was easier to handle. That's what a personal mission statement will do.

I have a vision board that I just worked on last week. It's the background of both my computer screens, my phone screen, and on my tablet. There is a question on the top of that vision board that says, "Is what you're doing today getting you closer to the goal that's ahead of you?" You see, having a goal is good, but a mission statement helps solidify "why" you're doing what you're doing.

While I didn't spend a lot of time on this part, I believe it's one of the most important things you can do in your life. Let me close out this chapter with something that I know will change your life forever. Consider this a free life hack. This "hack" is something I've seen work 100% of the time. As I've stated before, I am a professional people watcher. I love watching successful people from all walks of life. Someone once told me that it's okay to be a copycat as long as you're copying the right cat. This last little bit is something I've seen work with every single one of those professional people.

When creating your mission statement, you can't make it all about you. Your life has to become others-focused. As I've watched financially successful people, I've observed both people who've done this and who haven't. The ones who forget to be others-focused, the ones who make all about themselves, are usually the ones miserable. Yeah, they have a lot of money. They have tons of things money can buy, but they can't seem to buy that one thing that makes them happy. On the opposite end of the spectrum are the people who live their lives selflessly. They are the ones who are others-focused. It seems to work wonders in the lives of selfless people.

By being others-focused, something miraculous happens. Blessing, prosperity, happiness, and so much more becomes easier to achieve. It's like adding some kind of divine substance to the garden. The seeds planted will grow faster, fuller, and help the person change more lives in the process. When being others-focused, you have to ensure it's for the right reasons. I don't know why this works, but somehow it brings a lot more prosperity into the life of the selfless person. In the end, what does that person do? They use the platform, success, as a tool to help more people.

Take time to make your mission statement. Hang it up on the wall near your work area. Make sure you can see it every time you sit down to work. I promise you that doors will begin to open that you didn't even think was possible.

You've officially set yourself up to win. Let's get to winning by letting our imaginations flow. It's time to start writing your book!

Chapter 4:
Let's Get To Work!

We've successfully set ourselves up for success. Now it's time to start the process of getting everything out. When it comes to writing, most people get discouraged because they don't know what to write. A lot of people get so lost in the process of writing that they decide to quit. I've talked to several people who chose not to continue writing their books. When I asked them why they stopped, they all had the same thing to say.

"I loved writing when I was in school," one lady began to tell me. "I thought I still had it, you know, that love for writing. The problem is that I have no clue where to start."

This conversation came up one day while talking about my writing prompts. One of the things I love to do is to use writing prompts to help keep my imagination alive. Once I've found the writing prompt I want to use, I will start writing. I don't put any thought into it. Other authors have told me that this isn't normal, but I fear I make other "non-writers" feel like that's the way to do things. The lady I was talking to this day, who had just read several of my writing prompt stories, felt like she was inadequate.

"I don't think you've lost your love for writing," I told her. "Most likely, you're doing what I've done before. I'm great at writing prompts, but for a long time, I wasn't so good at things that required me to plot out."

What I laid out for her was the simple process of mind mapping and use that to create an outline. I've shared this with quite a few people. Most of them already knew on some level what mind mapping was. More than half of those people rolled their eyes, whether physically or mentally. For whatever reason, it seems that most people don't like the process of preparing. The idea of not preparing, or just winging an entire book is odd to me.

No author steps up to his desk and just starts writing a novel. They have to map out where the story will go. Most professional writers use mind mapping to write their books. What makes any of us "newbies" think that we don't have to? It doesn't make sense. Allow me to walk you through my favorite part of the writing process.

<u>Mind mapping</u>

For me, mind mapping is one of the most fun parts of the writing process. I honestly fully expected the process of doing it to be tedious and boring. For a while, I avoided it. I don't know if I mentioned this already or not, but procrastination has always been a thing for me. It was born out of laziness and fear, and it became far too easy to allow it to keep happening. Mind mapping was another procrastination moment for me. Finally, after many days of putting it aside, I decided to do it, and I'm glad I did.

Mind mapping is a visual thinking tool. It's a way of helping a writer structure their information which will allow them to analyze better, comprehend, recall, and generate fresh ideas.

There is a phrase that I think everyone has heard, especially if they're a person from the south as I am. This phrase is something I have to remind myself of all the time. The phrase is, "Keep it simple, stupid." I don't know if you have this problem, but I tend to overthink *everything*. There are a lot of moments when this comes in handy; I've learned to harness my overthinking for good. However, the reason I love mind mapping is that I intentionally keep it simple.

Mind mapping is also very rewarding for me to do. My favorite time to talk to my wife is when she has gone to bed after a busy day. It has kind of turned into a running joke between us. That, for some unknown reason, is when my mind comes alive. I'm a visionary by nature. Being a visionary usually means I get elaborate ideas to make the world a better place *all the time.* There is always a point in my rambling when I stop and say, "I've got to take a mind dump. Good night."

Go ahead and judge me. I know it's juvenile to call it that, but I think it's funny. I put a ton of information on my wall near my desk. I took anything and everything about what I was mind mapping and put it up there. Afterward, I realized I felt better; I felt relieved. Thus the term "mind dump" was born.

Let's go ahead and get into how to take a mind dump properly.

How to mind map

Before we get to the "how-to" portion of this, I want to give you my opinion on something. I believe sticking to the old fashioned way of mind mapping is the best way to go. I am somewhat of a techie. When it comes to new software, app, or device, I'm one of those people that want to put my hands on it. There has always been this desire to explore everything technology has to offer. However, I do NOT think to rely on technology when you're mind mapping is a good thing. Several apps allow you to mind map on your phone and computer. I've tried all of them in an attempt to find the perfect one. There was one major problem. None of the apps did what I needed them to do. They always came up short.

That's when I started using the method I am going to share with you now. First of all, this works so well because it's tangible. It allows you to put your hands on the very thing you're creating. That's what I think is missing when doing it digitally. It's easy not to see it. By doing it the way I choose to do it, you're going to look at your mind map every time you're at your desk.

All you're going to need for this is:
Notecards
Thumbtacks
A wall
Sandwich baggies

What I usually do it write down my topic and place it in the center of the wall. Titles don't matter, but I'll admit that I'm a sucker for a good title. Personally, there's something about being able to refer to the project by name that makes it feel more real. It's okay if you don't have a title. Most of the time, my title changes several times before I finish it.

The next thing you're going to do is think of at least six main topics. What is it you're trying to say about your main topic? What are the main points that you want people to take away from what you're writing? Figuring out your main topics will take some thought, but it'll be worth it. It doesn't matter what it is. If you have an idea, then put it on the wall. It's that easy.

Okay, I said "easy," but I realize that some people might not know where their structure is going. The people I find that have this problem are those writing about their lives. A lot of people, when writing nonfiction, only want to tell their story. Telling your story is excellent and will most likely help a lot of people. I love reading personal stories about triumph while facing "impossible" odds, but what I love more is a structured book that allows me to learn in the process. Teaching people life lessons, while at the same time telling your story, is something you want to think about when you're mind mapping. You want your book to leave people with the tools that allow them to say, "I can do that, too!"

The next thing you'll do from here is thinking of three main subtopics for each topic you've created. While doing this, you might see that one of the main topics would be better as a subtopic instead. It's your book, your mind map, so structure how you want. You will be moving a lot of things around, and that's okay.

I want to teach you from my mistakes. One of the things I do a lot during the mind mapping process is not putting enough detail on the notecard. I usually generalize and say, "Oh, I know what that means." Guess what happens? Yep, you guessed it. I almost ALWAYS forget. I have another book I will be working on soon. One of the subtopics on my wall says, "headache." Most likely, it is going to be a great point and will be the greatest thing ever put in a book. There is one major problem. I've been trying to think of what it means for over a week now. I have no clue and had to put it to the side.

Something else you'll do while mind mapping is include a random section for topics that might not fit immediately. As you begin to think of subtopics and put everything in its place, you'll think of something you want to include, but you won't know where to put it. No problem. Just put it in a random section. Some of those things you will use later.

Now you've got a messy looking mind map on your wall. That might give you anxiety, but I assure you everything is going to work out just fine. My wife said that my messiness is most peoples organized. I like having an order to things. One of the things I've noticed is that people with clutters everywhere are usually cluttered in a lot of other areas (finances, family, etc.). I guess I'm suggesting that you put a little order to everything, so you don't get too overwhelmed in the process.

<u>Must have order!</u>

The next thing we are going to do is find some order amid our chaos. Finding order the way I do is where some people think I'm taking it too far, but the people who do this seem to have a better chance of completing their books. You're going to start taking everything down. You're going to need your sandwich bags for this process.

Grab your main topic and put the subtopics behind it. You'll put each topic and the subtopics in a bag. It's important to keep your main topic facing out where you can read it. The random subtopics will have its bag as well. Do this for all your topics until the only notecard on your wall is the title.

Take your title card and put it at the top of your wall. Also, this would be an excellent time to remind you of your mission statement. Put that somewhere next to your title. It's important to see that through the entire process of writing your book. I've stressed this before, but that mission statement will motivate you during times when you want to give up. Maybe you're some super-duper person who never has doubts, but if you're like the rest of us humans, you'll have moments of wanting to quit. Look at your mission statement.

Underneath your title going across will be all of your main topics. Go through each one and decide the order. When you pin each topic you'll also be putting the subtopics underneath. You'll want to loosely figure out what order you want those to be in, too. Doing this takes a little bit of time, but you'll be thankful you did this. Don't move on to the next topic until you've finished the one your own. It's easy to want to jump ahead and assume you can come back to what you were doing. Don't risk losing any momentum. As you continue doing this, you'll begin to see your structure; your book is taking shape. Putting everything in its proper place, finding order, is why I love mind mapping the most. I get to see my book long before words are on a page.

When I start the chapters (aka the main topics), I use colored note cards. I know this is a waste of paper for all the old ones, but I like to color coordinate. It's aesthetically pleasing, but it also helps keep each chapter from spilling over into the next.

Let's bust out the computer!

Remember how I said I could be a little obsessive about things? This is another one of those moments, but I assure you it works wonders. We are getting closer to writing, but we need to put everything in its place first. In other words, we are putting the mind map into written form. I don't feel like this is overkill. The work you put in now is setting you up to win. You'll be setting yourself up to win more than most people.

On your computer, you're going to create a folder. Name it whatever you want just as long as you know this is only for your book. Inside that folder, create additional folders for each chapter. I have found that creating separate folders for each one works best. It's really easy to get overwhelmed with the whole process of finding the things you need for what you're writing.

From here is when you're going to create an outline for each chapter. Creating this outline is so easy because you will be taking what's on your wall and putting it into outline form. Open whatever word program you have and begin to put it down. While you're doing this, you might see that a few things need to be changed. Maybe you'll want to add a few additional notes so you don't lose what you want to say. Because you have separate folders, each chapter will have its word document.

Once you've completed each chapter, it will be time to move onto the research. One of the things writers are guilty of is doing too much research instead of writing. What we are going to do is eliminate this as a possibility as much as we can. Each chapter will have its research document in it. As you go through your outline in each section, begin to think about what you'll need for research. It's better to have too much than not enough. In your research document, include the link to any sites you find. If it's a book you need to reference, then add what book and the page number. Find a way to mark the page and spot in the book, too. You don't want to waste valuable time looking for something you need.

Research is essential but can be time-consuming. Put in the work now. Not doing proper research before you start writing is a mistake beginning authors make. Countless hours will go to research instead of doing what you're supposed to be doing. Newton's first law of motion says that an object at rest stays at rest and an object in motion stays in motion. I'm not a scholar in the area of physics, but what I do know is research can ofttimes be the motion killer. It's incredibly challenging to get back into the groove of things after you've spent so much time away from writing.

I've had plenty of times when I needed to do additional research, but I didn't want to waste too much time doing it. What I've learned to do is to leave a bold note in my document in red that says, "Research goes here." I will jot down on a piece of paper where I need the research. Once I've gotten ready to close out the days writing, I will find what I needed, then go back and add it. No time wasted; I stayed in motion.

Chapter 5:
Let's Write!

Getting to this point has taken some work, but it's going to pay off. It's time to write your book. One of the things you'll notice about this book is that it has very little in it about writing. Everything thus far has been about setting yourself up to write. I've said it before, but it's worth repeating. Setting yourself up to win is, in my humble opinion, one of the most important things you'll do. I'm passionate about that because it's those things I've shared with you already that's helped others finish what they started. You do have to write, though. So *how* does one do that?

Sit down.
Get on your computer.
And WRITE!

Is that a little too easy for you? Were you looking for more? I know that so many people have that question. Once again, you've done the work required to write. Seriously, your outline is everything you'll need. If, for some reason, you need a little more help getting to the point of writing, then here is some additional advice.

Start with your first chapter and pull up your outline. Go through your outline and write a paragraph or two about what each bullet point will include. Writing that little bit helps get the creative juices flowing. You know what? Most likely, you won't have to do that. You'll start to; then the realization will hit you that you might as well just start writing. Thanks to your outline, you already have everything you need. Adding meat to the bones is easy.

I feel like a better thing to cover during the writing portion of this book is the roadblocks you will most likely face. These are things that almost all authors have encountered at one point or another. I've watched interviews with some famous authors who've said they still have doubts about what they write. What I am trying to tell you is that you're in good company if you face any of the things we are about to discuss.

Roadblocks

Roadblocks seem to pop up when we least expect them. I wrote 5,000 words the other day and encountered a significant roadblock. I let it win for a little bit. Through the last few years, I've heard some wonderfully constructed excuses as to why the person didn't finish their writing. Usually, the person will start strong, but something will happen that'll make them derail. There is always a great reason, but I know it's because they faced a roadblock. They didn't confront it properly. Because of this, they quit. You and I will never get to read their book.

Time

If I made a list of reasons why people don't write or end up quitting, the excuse of time would be #1 on that list. I would sum up the excuse of time in one statement. "I don't have enough time" is what so many people are telling me. Why does this irritate me so much? It's because I know they're telling me a big fat lie. Time is usually not a valid lie. If what you want to write is important enough, then you'll find the time.

The best way to conquer this time excuse is to make a schedule. It was my wife that helped me see this. I was guilty of just winging it. Consequently, I was never getting anything done. I mean, there were a few things here and there that I was able to finish, but never any big projects.

What I had to do was make a schedule. To successfully do this, you'll have to be truthful with yourself. Evaluate where your time is going. I was able to see all the time I was wasting binge watching Netflix or YouTube videos. Making a schedule, actually paying attention to where your time is going, will be a major eye-opener. If you absolutely must watch something, then add it to your schedule. Commit not to go over your allotted time for watching a show or movie.

When making a schedule, it's also good to remember your why. Look at your mission statement. Is what you're writing worth the sacrifice of not watching a show? There are things you have to include in your schedule. Time with family is essential. I would suggest not letting your time with family be taken away by a screen. Spend time with your family, but also remember that your schedule is vital. If you need to work with a loved one to help with this, then do that. Make sure everyone else is on the same page. You have to make sure other people in the house respect your time.

Another thing about setting up a schedule is that you're getting into the habit of writing. Once it becomes a habit, you'll notice that writing becomes more natural. You'll begin to establish a pattern of writing at a specific time. Make sure to adhere to that schedule.

You'll need to make exceptions. All of us have those moments when creativity hits, and we need to write. If you're feeling it and it's not "time" to write, then, by all means, sit down and get it done. I have tons of moments when my mind begins to run wild with ideas. My wife knows when it happens because I won't stop talking when it's time to go to bed. I will get up, go to my computer, and let the creativity flow.

Time is your friend, not your enemy. Set a schedule, but be open to working when the creativity hits.

Family and friends

Okay, saying that a roadblock could be your family and friends sounds rude. I'm a man who enjoys isolation. So I was cautious about even touching on this topic. We addressed it briefly when it comes to managing time. Because it's easy for me to isolate, which is something I'm still working on correcting, my wife will let me know when I need to take a break. I joke about this a lot with her and refer to is a "humaning." I don't think that's a word, but for those of us who enjoy being by ourselves, humaning is a very real thing.

A roadblock for you might be that you're not spending enough time with family. Yes, writing your book is very important, but you need to make sure to make time for your family. Technically speaking, this helps your overall brain health. Spending time with them will help you disengage from what you're doing and release some of the feel-good chemicals in your brain. In other words, you need interaction with your family.

On the flip side, some people let their family become a distraction in a way that they never get any writing done. Look, I know every situation is different. I get it. Your family and friends are important to you. I would argue that your story and the impact it could have to help people is also important. You have to make sure to include your family and friends in the process. I love finishing a few hours of writing and going to my wife to say, "I just wrote five thousand words. That makes a total of..." By including your family and friends in the process of writing, they will understand how important this is to you.

My wife is amazing in every way. She helps me balance my work as an author, and my time with my family. Remember that litter of children we have? Having this small army makes it difficult to find any time to get things done. Also, because my desk is in the dining room, it could be a recipe for disaster. My wife has become the enforcer of my time. She will make sure the kids stay away. Because of this, the kids know when I am working. Everyone is now on the same page. Learning to balance everything, having everyone on the same page, makes it easier for me to get things done. I don't have to feel guilty about working. There is a perfect balance of work and family time.

In all fairness, I have to include another group of people. These are the people who just don't see the work we do as...well work. I have a couple of friends who just don't get it. Do you know what I do? I don't spend as much time with them while I'm working. I can't afford their negativity. These people have learned that while I'm writing, my time with them is limited. There will be a few people you'll need to create some distance with, and that's okay. It's not that they aren't good friends. It's just that they will become a distraction. I've allowed these people to keep me down at times. Trust me when I say spending limited time with them while you're working will save you a lot of heartache in the future.

<u>Writer's Block Again?</u>

One of the most common roadblocks that all authors face is writer's block. A few years ago, I was going through a lot in my life. It seemed like everything around me was falling apart. Consequently, it became incredibly difficult to put anything down on paper. One of my loves in life is short stories. When I was in high school, writing short stories saved my life. Because it means so much to me, I've always made sure to incorporate writing into my weekly habits. I've always been okay with it not being a daily habit if I'm not working on a book or specific short story for a website. Everything was great until the writer's block hit. I shed tears over not being able to write.

Months went by, and I hadn't written anything. I was heartbroken. I wasn't quite sure what gave me the gift of writing the short stories that I love so much, but whatever it is was broken. There was no denying it. I was never going to write again.

One of my closest friends looked at me and said, "You're in your head too much. Look at the barista over there. What character would he be in a story of yours?"

Because there was no pressure, I came up with a story idea. Both of us got slightly emotional as the story unfolded. I did it without thinking about it. My friend then looked at me and said, "See? You don't have writer's block. You're just distracted on the crap. Now go write."

Jennifer Egan, an American novelist and short-story writer, said, "I haven't had writer's block. I think it's because my process involves writing very badly."

That is one of my favorite quotes because it helps sum up what I now think about writer's block. I didn't suffer from writer's block. What I suffered from was being overwhelmed by the things around me. I needed to unplug from all of those things and allow myself to get lost in the writing process. Writing does include writing "very badly," as Jennifer Egan said.

Since my days of writer's block, I've never dealt with it again. Have I had moments when it was difficult? Of course I have! Guess what came out of those moments? There were some diamonds in the rough. There was also a lot of coal that took some work to become diamonds. But what I've never done is allow writer's block to overtake me. After struggling with it several times, I've come to realize that it's almost always rooted in something going on in my life.

You're going to face a moment like this at some point or another. My suggestion is to work out what is causing it. Identifying the problem will help you move past it in a way that allows you to write. If it's something significant, then address it. Let it be a big deal. I'm not saying to minimize the problems in your life. What I am saying is that you can find a way to work through writer's block. Write, no matter what! I can't stress that enough. The moments I worked through "writer's block" were sometimes more rewarding than when it freely flowed. There is a beautiful feeling in knowing we've conquered that moment and produced something. So what if it's a lump of coal? You can go back and work on that.

Losing discipline or desire to write

For me, losing discipline or the desire to write happens a lot more than it should. Short stories are incredibly easy for me. However, there have been several times when I was writing nonfiction for a website. In the middle of writing it, I will lose interest; my desire to write will be at an all-time low. This loss of attention happens to the best of us, especially when we are writing nonfiction. The idea of writing out story sounds epic. The execution of writing our story gets a little boring. And by "a little," I mean "a lot."

The goal of this book is to help you tell your story no matter what. Writing your book is a huge undertaking. The excitement of writing your story will wear off. Okay, maybe your some kind of superhuman who won't have this issue. For the rest of us meer mortals writing our story will lose its luster. I think that's natural. You've spent so much time prepping, and maybe at this point, you've written quite a bit. The monotony of writing begins to get to you. So what do you do?

First, I think it is to remember that it could be because you're not used to writing every day. You've never written a book before. Having a mindset geared towards writing for countless hours isn't something that comes naturally. It goes against almost everything you've done before now. Spending all that time writing isn't how you usually spend your time. When it comes to losing interest, your reader will tell if you were just forcing something to get it out there. You have to find ways of keeping yourself motivated.

When this happens to me, there are a few things I do.

1. I will look at my mission statement(s). Because I've attached my feelings to it finding motivation isn't that difficult.

2. I talk to someone about my lack of motivation. My wife is the world's best at building me up. She will remind me of my awesomeness, and I will walk away, feeling like Superman has nothing on me.

3. I will work on something about the book, but it might not be actual writing. Sometimes this is merely going through and reviewing my research.

4. I will start getting pumped up. I have a DVD set of all Michael Jordan's movies. I love going back and watching what he accomplished. Sometimes I will look up the top 10 best dunks of whatever year. Seeing those gets me excited. However you have to find your excitement, as long as it's healthily, it is a good thing. Find your outlet. You'll thank me later.

Doubt

I saved self-doubt for last because it's such a soul-crushing problem that a lot of people deal with on an almost constant basis. Do you know why I know this one is a big hitter? Take this book as an example. I know that what I'm sharing has helped plenty of people in the past. However, I've doubted writing this book at least 1,000,935.8 times. I was shocked to read about successful authors dealing with this even though they've had tremendous success. In a 2014 interview with Rolling Stone, Stephen King said, "I'm afraid of failing at whatever story I'm writing – that it won't come up for me, or that I won't be able to finish it." If STEPHEN FREAKING

KING struggles with doubt, then it's safe to say that you might deal with it, too. It's what we do with that doubt that matters.

One of the first doubts I had came in the form of a question to my wife. "What if what I'm writing isn't good enough?" I feel like that's a question a lot of other authors have asked and allowed it to deter them from finishing what they started. Nobody is immune to self-doubt. What I know is that if you deal with this, then you can find a way to fight through it.

I know this is going to sound like some self-help guru kind of stuff, but you have to see yourself as worth it. What I always fall back on when I am doubting myself is thinking about the people I will help. This book covers some pretty basic stuff. I know it does. Because of that, I've been afraid of the brutal comments that will most likely come from the people who can't see the bigger picture. It's easy for me to allow that fear to creep in and allow it to rob me of my positive self-image. Most of the time, all it takes is for me to remember that I am not alone.

The truth is that I've allowed doubt to rob me for many years. It's all I've known most of my life. Transitioning from that broken mindset to someone who is a confident writer hasn't been easy. Even while writing this, I made sure to keep writing. Wow, that's an ugly sentence. I mean that I continued to force myself to write. I had to fight through the doubt of this book not being good enough. I was determined not to quit. Admittedly I did delete a lot in the beginning. I had to start over a couple of times because I let the fear win. I can't stress to you that you're not alone in the battle of self-doubt.

There is another quote I love that is from Stephen King in his book On Writing. He said, "I have spent a good many years—too many, I think—being ashamed about what I write. I kept hearing Miss Hisler asking why I wanted to waste my talent, why I wanted to waste my time, why I wanted to write junk. I think I was forty before I realized that almost every writer of fiction and poetry who has ever published a line has been accused by someone of wasting his or her God-given talent."

The reason I am using Stephen King as an example is that he is an author that everyone knows. He's had a success story that most authors dream of knowing they'll never achieve that kind of greatness. Being such a gifted author, one could assume he is somehow immune to doubt. That's farther from the truth. He is human, just like all of us. Do you know what he did that you need to do as well? You've got to write through the self-doubt.

One of the most significant ways I conquered self-doubt when it started growing was to write. Yep, it's that easy. Okay, maybe "easy" isn't the way to put it. It's exhausting, and clicking on the delete option seems like it's the best thing to do. I'm guilty of deleting a lot of things. It's something my wife gets on to me about almost weekly. I've learned that there is power in just pushing through.

I can't promise that your book is going to crush it when it's released. It might not be a best-seller. What I can promise you is that it will help someone. One of the greatest legacies I want to leave on this earth when I die is knowing I changed as many lives as I could. I feel like our world has become too self-absorbed. What we need are books that will make the world a better place.

What we need is *Your First Book.*

Now that we've talked about the roadblocks that will most likely present themselves, I think it's good we cover a few final tips and tricks that'll make your writing experience a little better.

Tips and tricks

Now that we reside in the modern era where technology is king, I feel there are a few things that will help you. I don't think any of these little tricks are mind-blowing things you don't know, but most of us forget about this when we start. I still forget some of these. So I am sharing from my shortcomings and discoveries along the way.

When I open a document, there is one setting that is now automatic, red underlining. I'm personally a massive fan of the red underline, but it can become distracting while you're writing. Seeing will make you want to stop writing so you can go back to correct it. I feel that undoing this in whatever program you're using will save you some time. You can always go back and edit later.

Eliminating the cute little red underline brings me to the next lesson that I do far too much when writing. Do NOT attempt to edit while you're writing. Your job in writing *Your First Book,* and the purpose of this book, is to help you finish your rough draft. Finishing a rough draft is something most beginning authors don't complete. Their idea for a book remains to be just that...an idea. Editing is something you can do once you've written each chapter. That's why I like keeping each chapter separated into their document. It's easier to edit one section at a time than all of it at once.

While we are on the subject of editing, I think it's good to introduce you to what can become your best friend. There is a program called Grammarly that you can install on every device you have. The free version is usually all anyone should need. However, the people who've paid for the subscription seem to like it. It's never full proof, but it will save you a lot of time editing since it finds almost all of the errors for you. I suggest using the free version than having someone else read through it.

Another tip that's helped me immensely is turning off my internet. Having access to the internet might not seem like that big of a deal, but I've found it to save me a lot of time. It took me a while to incorporate this into my writing habits. Finally, I broke down and took the advice of another author. Upon doing this, it didn't take me too long to see how much time I'd been wasting doing other things on my computer. The only thing I will turn it on for is to look up whatever research I need; then, I will turn it off again. I'm so glad I listened to this advice, and you will be, too.

This next bit of advice comes with some hesitance. I've had people debate this. There are also articles online that try and explain why this next thing is good. My opinion is that this is not debatable. So here it is: clean up your workspace. Seriously! Having a cluttered area isn't healthy for your overall mental health. Your brain will instinctively associate that clutter as normal and translate that into every other area of your life. I've proven this in the lives of several people when I put them to the clutter-free lifestyle. Seasonal depression was minimal. They were more productive. Eliminating this as a problem is worth taking the time to be clean. No clutter! Clutter = bad!

Phones are also a significant distraction. The way our cellular devices rule our lives is disturbing. I have moments when I need to get out and do some "humaning." When I go to the cafe near me, I always see the same thing. Almost all the people in the place are looking down at their phones. Mindlessly staring at my phone is something I'm guilty of, too. I'm annoyed with how much I look at my phone. My suggestion for writing isn't to put your phone on airplane mode as most others suggest. Instead, put your phone on vibrate and put it face down on your desk. Ridding yourself of the distractions of your phone makes it easier to get work done. If, for some reason, you need to have access to it, then having it on vibrate allows you to quickly glance at it to ensure everything is okay. I promise you that one Twitter, Facebook, or Instagram comment isn't that important.

Lastly, the tip I would give you that'll help you maintain a healthy writing life is to schedule in your breaks. I don't think it's healthy to write for hours on end without a break. Just a few minutes ago, I stood up, walked around, and talked to my wife. It was a nice break. I find it best to create a good stopping point in what I'm writing instead of making it a specific time. You don't want to take a break while you're in the flow and cranking out some words. Find your stopping point and take a quick little break. It's good for your brain and will allow you to accomplish more.

Armed with everything I've given you up to this point will set you up to finish *Your First Book.* I know you're still going to be overwhelmed, but I assure you that you'll be able to write your book successfully if you follow your outline and know how to maneuver through the roadblocks that present themselves. In the next and final chapter, I will give you some additional information that'll help you get closer to the self-publishing part.

Chapter 6:
Finishing Touches

The purpose of this book was to teach you how to set yourself up to win when it came time to write *Your First Book*. I debated whether or not I would include anything about publishing, but it seems too important to not at least cover some of the basics. This part is not as difficult as most people make it. I mean, it's not always "easy," but I hope you'll see there are plenty of options to make *Your First Book* the perfect book.

There are things that you might worry about while you're in the writing process. As a beginning author, I often wondered how people with limited financial resources were able to do everything. How do they get the cover to look so good? Are they hiring a graphic artist? Where do they find an editor? Do I need a publisher? I had so many questions.

Self-publishing

Almost everyone who is starting their first book is wondering what publisher they should choose. I used to have the same thought. Allow me to introduce you to the wonderful world of self-publishing. Before Amazon and other companies like them existed, everyone had to use a publisher. The primary problem with a publisher is that they won't always have your best interest in mind. In most cases, as I've read, they are just trying to break even. Then the internet was born.

Perfectly gift-wrapped by God was this fantastic thing called the internet. Today it's become an addiction to many. However, some businesses made the best of the new resource and chose to dominate.

You can now write, edit, create a book cover, and post your book all from the comforts of your computer. I'm old enough to remember when the greatest technology was the first Nintendo, and young me was convinced we had peaked. There was no way it could get any better. Boy! Was I ever wrong!

Self-publishing is one of the greatest ways to get your book out there, especially today. By doing everything yourself, you can ensure that you'll set yourself to be more of a success. I feel like posting your books via Kindle is one of the most powerful, easiest, and quickest ways to get your book in people's hands. Amazon is quite brilliant in that a person doesn't have to have a Kindle to download and read a book. You can download the app on almost every device that has access to the internet. That means *billions* of devices are out there with the capability to download your book! WOW!

When it comes to being a self-published author, you have a lot more freedom to create the perfect book. With a publisher, you're selling the rights to your book. Selling the rights means they can change the name, cover, and so much more without asking you. That doesn't sound so appealing to me.

Self-publishing is the way to go, and there are a lot of successful authors who are doing it.

Editing

No matter how well I think I've written, it's always a guarantee that I will have missed a lot of mistakes. I've learned to stop worrying about the errors and let the creativity flow. The problem is that I use passive voice a lot, and I still don't understand what that is when I'm doing it. I type out horribly constructed sentences. I make a lot of mistakes. One of the things I knew I would need is an editor. But where do I find one? That's such a great question that if you search for it will send you to 1,000's of sites. It's too overwhelming, to say the least.

There are a few places you can go to have your book edited. Those places are **www.guru.com**, **www.fiverr.com**, and **www.upwork.com**. These three places have plenty of people to choose from and are somewhat easy to use. The beauty is that these people are willing to work with you even more than a publisher would. You'll be getting professional results at a tiny fraction of the price. That's a win for anyone.

Something else you'll want to invest in is a program like Grammarly. The free version works very well. However, paying for the extra is well worth it. Trust me. You'll thank me later.

<u>Book cover</u>

Whether in a book store or browsing in Amazon, the book cover is the first thing that catches a person's eye. If you don't have a good enough book cover, then you'll lose out on sales. Is that enough pressure for you? I promise that it's not that difficult.

When people look at a book, they usually read the cover from the top left, working their way down. Knowing this patter means that you want your title to be in their face; it needs to be the first thing they notice. Then from there, they will read the subtitle. Your title has to be catchy enough, while the subtitle needs to relay what they are getting from your book. I've read a cover of a self-help book and had no clue what the book was even about.

It's good to have an idea of how you want the cover to look. The same resources are available that I mentioned above (**www.guru.com**,

www.fiverr.com, **www.upwork.com**), but there is another option you can use that is free. When I wrote this book, I wanted to include a cover using this resource to prove that you don't have to go to great lengths and seek someone out. The site I used was **www.canva.com**. I selected the book cover option, chose a template, did some minor tweaking, and the cover of this book was the result. I'm a firm believer that as long as it looks professional and your content is good, then your book is going to sell and make a lot of people happy they read it.

If you do not want to do it yourself, then you can seek out someone to do it for you. Most people have had the best results by going to **www.fiverr.com**. That site started with the idea of getting things done for only $5. The site was a lot of fun, but it has grown considerably. From what I've heard from others, you can get a great book cover design done for around $40, and they will have examples of their previous work. You'll know what you're getting before you hire them for your book cover.

<u>Campaigns</u>

Promoting your book is the one thing that can seem the most aggravating. Most authors I've chatted with who utilize the proper tools seem to love the process of promoting more than the writing. The reason people love it is because they're growing an audience that will help them later. They utilize the almighty email list. There are authors, and plenty of other professionals, who say a person will live or die by the email list. An email list will allow you to get positive reviews when your book is published. Having an excited audience of people who support you is a life changer. Most of the people on your list are going to be people you don't know. Keep that in mind as you start sharing information. Creating a successful book campaign is something I am still working on, but let me give you the two most powerful tools out there.

Two platforms help you create email campaigns that most professionals use. Those are **www.mailchimp.com** and **www.mailerlite.com**. Once you start generating traffic, you will have to upgrade to a paid plan. I would suggest you play around with each one and figure out what fits you. I've enjoyed using Mail Chimp and have referred several people over there. However, I know people who've made the switch over to the other.

Once you've set that up, you're going to want to set up an account with **www.bookfunnel.com**. This site allows you to run campaigns that will help generate traffic to your email list. Usually, people will include a free digital copy (pdf) of their book as long as they sign up for the mailing list. While giving away your book for free might not make a lot of sense, I assure you it will be worth it. It's something that will pay off later.

The next thing you'll need to do is create a social media presence long before the book comes out. Creating a social media presence will be done on Facebook, Twitter, Instagram, and possibly LinkedIn. I'm not a massive fan of social media and have been able to live through my wife. I've always enjoyed the privacy. I'm slowly heeding my advice and joining because almost every person I know says I need to consider using it. Maybe I'll get there eventually. Anyway, on Facebook, you'll want to create a business page as an author. Invite every person on your friend's list to join your page. Also, find a few close friends who are willing to do the same thing. You'll begin to get an immediate following.

Once you've got your page up and going, you'll want to be faithful with posting on your page. Keep your name in front of people. Start doing fun things like asking random fun questions that keep them commenting. Another thing to do is maybe to design two different covers for your book. Have everyone vote on which is their favorite. It's good to make people feel like they're a part of the process. Lastly, consider offering a chapter of your book for free when they join your page. You can also use your Facebook page to run your campaign for the free book.

Another tool with Facebook is that they allow paying for ads. What I love about it is that you can pick how much you want to spend, what kind of person you're looking for, what region, and so much more. Running a campaign becomes fun and rewarding because you'll have more people joining your email list.

Once you've officially launched your book, you'll ask everyone on your email list to download it from Amazon, read the final draft, and leave a five-star review with a positive comment. People read the comments. I know I do. I want to know what people are saying about the book before I purchase it.

Kindle Direct Publishing

There is far too much to include here. When it comes to publishing your book, I would have to write another book just to cover everything. What I can tell you is that Amazon has got you covered. No matter what questions you have, they have already answered them.

The best thing to do when you're ready to publish your book is to go to **www.kdp.com**. That link will take you to the Kindle Direct Publishing (KDP) page. Create an account and begin to browse around. KDP isn't as intimidating as you would think. They have questions and answers that will cover almost anything you could think of about posting your book.

A suggestion I would give is to know your price point. Something to consider is whether you want 35% or 70%. I know that might seem like a stupid statement because all of us want a higher percentage. Amazon will give you 70% of every book you sell as long as it's between the prices of $2.99 and $9.99. Anything below that or above that will only receive 35% of the total price. It's best to keep within the 70% range unless you're running a temporary promotion.

Lastly is that you might want to consider Kindle Unlimited. Kindle Unlimited is a plan that people sign up for, and it's terrific. I've had it for a while now, and I enjoy it. Kindle Unlimited pays between $.004 and $.005 per page. Now I know that doesn't sound like a lot, but if you're looking to publish more than one book, then this is an option that will eventually pay off. I was chatting with another author two weeks ago who said he makes more through Kindle Unlimited than he does through his other sales. That's mind-blowing to me, but he also has quite a few books posted.

Final thoughts

As you can see, there is a lot to take in when it comes to publishing. My hope in writing this book is that you would find the tools you need to set yourself up for success. Writing a book is a long and sometimes tiring process. As I stated before, more people fail to complete writing their books than the ones that do. I want you to finish your book and be proud of what you produced.

Thank you for trusting me with your time as you've read this book. If this book has helped you, then please go on Amazon and leave me a review. (See what I did there? I have to get reviews.)

As you finish your book, I would love to read it. Feel free to email me at **MikeDMcLeod@gmail.com**

Send me pictures of what you've accomplished along the way. Tag me on Instagram (@mikemcleodwrites) and let me know you read my book. Follow me because I'm new to the social media game. I feel like Instagram is the most rewarding to keep up with what you're doing.

I look forward to reading *Your First Book*.

www.ingramcontent.com/pod-product-compliance
Lightning Source LLC
Chambersburg PA
CBHW051229250726
48655CB00006B/2675